INVENTIONS THAT CHANGED THE WORLD
THE TELEPHONE

BY SARA GREEN

Bellwether Media • Minneapolis, MN

Blastoff! Discovery launches a new mission: reading to learn. Filled with facts and features, each book offers you an exciting new world to explore!

This edition first published in 2022 by Bellwether Media, Inc.

No part of this publication may be reproduced in whole or in part without written permission of the publisher.
For information regarding permission, write to Bellwether Media, Inc., Attention: Permissions Department,
6012 Blue Circle Drive, Minnetonka, MN 55343.

Library of Congress Cataloging-in-Publication Data

LC record for The Telephone available at: https://lccn.loc.gov/2021049234

Text copyright © 2022 by Bellwether Media, Inc. BLASTOFF! DISCOVERY and associated logos are trademarks and/or registered trademarks of Bellwether Media, Inc.

Editor: Rebecca Sabelko   Designer: Josh Brink

Printed in the United States of America, North Mankato, MN.

TABLE OF CONTENTS

STUDY TIME! 4

A BETTER WAY TO COMMUNICATE 8

THE RISE OF SMARTPHONES 22

A SMART FUTURE 26

TELEPHONE TIMELINE 28

GLOSSARY 30

TO LEARN MORE 31

INDEX 32

STUDY TIME!

The big science project is due tomorrow! A group of friends decides to work in the library after school. They pull out their smartphones to text their parents for permission.

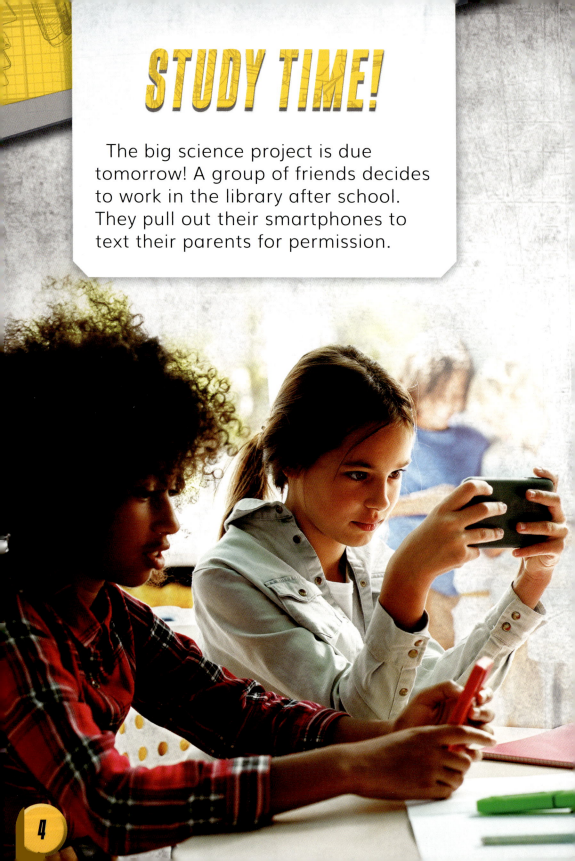

The friends check texts and emails while waiting to hear back. Finally, their smartphones buzz. Their parents said yes! The students reserve a study room on the library's **app**. They tell their smartphones to add reminders.

The final school bell rings. The friends' smartphones remind them about the meeting. They grab their books and head to the library. Once they arrive, they open the library app and check in. Time to work!

The friends are building a car for their science project. They get out all of their supplies. They use their smartphones to look up solutions to problems as they build their car. Before long, they are done. Smartphones made completing their science project easy!

A BETTER WAY TO COMMUNICATE

Before the telephone was invented, it was more difficult to communicate with people who were far away. People often lived far apart. They wrote letters, but mail delivery could take weeks or longer.

DID YOU KNOW?
From April 1860 to October 1861, the Pony Express delivered mail and news to the western United States. The nearly 2,000-mile (3,219-kilometer) route took about 10 days to cover.

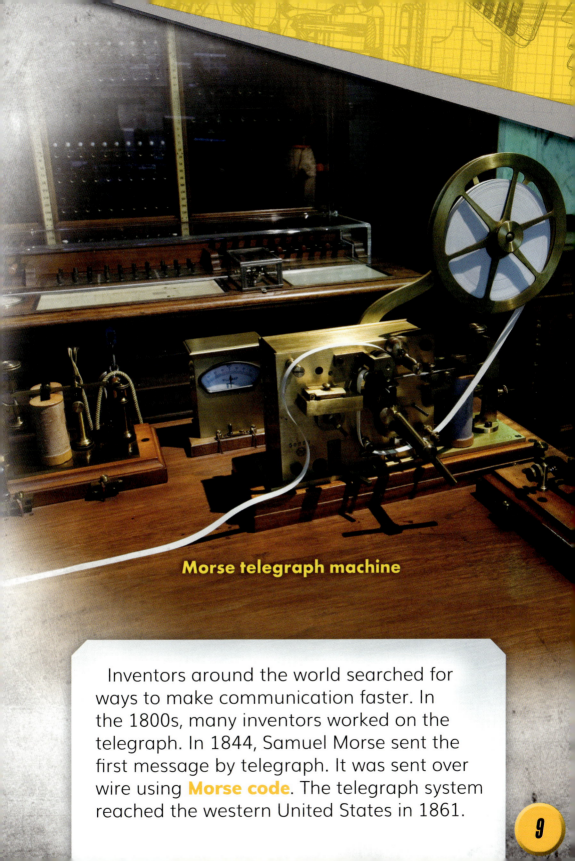

Morse telegraph machine

Inventors around the world searched for ways to make communication faster. In the 1800s, many inventors worked on the telegraph. In 1844, Samuel Morse sent the first message by telegraph. It was sent over wire using **Morse code**. The telegraph system reached the western United States in 1861.

Telegraphs helped people communicate over long distances. But sending messages was not easy. People did not have telegraphs in their homes, and most people did not know Morse code. To send messages, people had to go to telegraph offices. An **operator** tapped messages into a telegraph machine.

telegraph office

Antonio Meucci

Inventors continued to seek better ways for people to communicate. In 1849, Antonio Meucci designed a device that sent sounds across a wire. He called it a "talking telegraph." Meucci also invented other telephone-like devices. However, he could never afford to buy a **patent**.

Elisha Gray and Alexander Graham Bell also invented telephone devices. Both inventions used a liquid **transmitter** to change sound into electrical signals. On February 14, 1876, both men filed for patents for their inventions at an office in Washington, D.C. Bell arrived first and received the patent.

Bell's first telephone was called the box telephone. Box telephones were mounted to a wall or a table. The **receiver** and transmitter were paired together. The same opening was used for speaking and listening! Ringers were soon added to alert people to incoming calls.

box telephones

ALEXANDER GRAHAM BELL

Born: March 3, 1847, in Edinburgh, Scotland
Died: August 2, 1922
Background: Inventor who studied speech and the human voice
Invented: Telephone
Year Patented: 1876
Idea Development: Bell was working on inventing a telegraph that sent voice signals down a wire. He hired Thomas Watson as his assistant. The first words that Bell said on the telephone were, "Mr. Watson, come here. I want to see you."

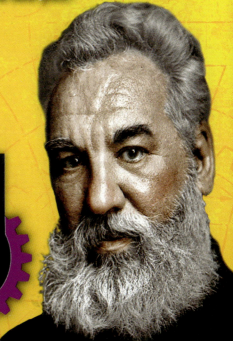

DID YOU KNOW?

Alexander Graham Bell wanted people to say "Ahoy" when they answered the phone. Inventor Thomas Edison suggested "Hello."

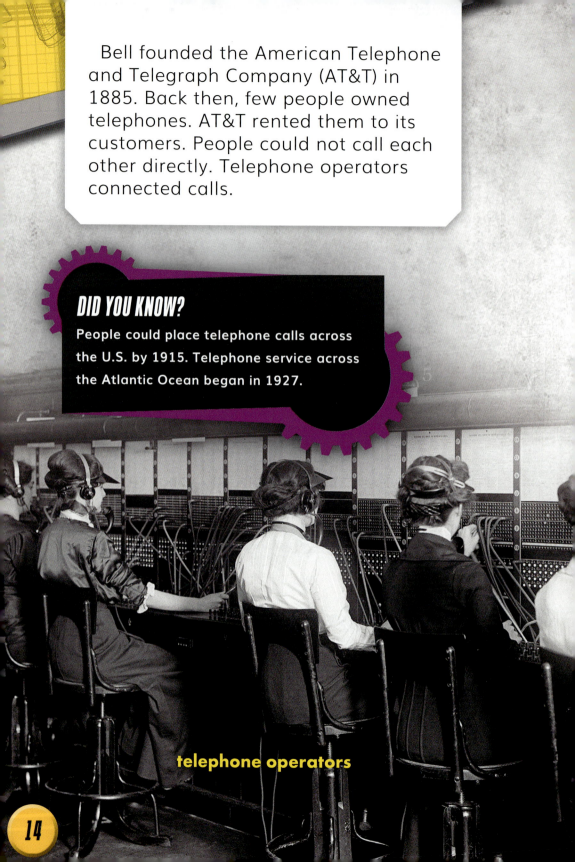

Bell founded the American Telephone and Telegraph Company (AT&T) in 1885. Back then, few people owned telephones. AT&T rented them to its customers. People could not call each other directly. Telephone operators connected calls.

DID YOU KNOW?

People could place telephone calls across the U.S. by 1915. Telephone service across the Atlantic Ocean began in 1927.

telephone operators

candlestick with rotary dial

Western Electric 102 B1 with rotary dial

Telephone technology advanced quickly. Upright phones called candlesticks debuted in the 1890s. Callers held mouthpieces in one hand and receivers in the other. **Rotary** dials were introduced in 1919. These phones allowed people to make direct calls without an operator. The Western Electric 102 **handset** debuted in 1927. It freed up one hand during calls!

The Western Electric 302 desk telephone debuted in 1937. It was the first popular telephone to have a ringer inside it. The 302 was upgraded to the Model 500 around 1950. This telephone came in a variety of colors. The Model 500 was the top-selling phone for decades!

Western Electric 302

Model 500

DID YOU KNOW?

Sales of cordless phones skyrocketed in the 1980s. They let people wander around the house and talk on the phone at the same time.

AT&T introduced the Princess phone in 1959. It was a smaller phone with a lighted dial. Touch-tone dials debuted in 1963. They allowed people to press buttons to call instead of using a rotary. The Western Electric Trimline, released in 1965, had a touch-tone dial in the handset. Millions of Trimlines were sold over time!

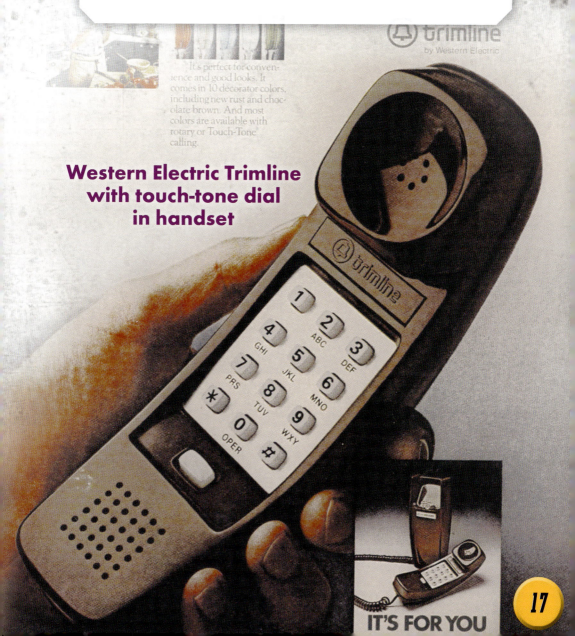

Western Electric Trimline with touch-tone dial in handset

The Motorola Company invented the first **cellular phone**, or cell phone, in 1973. It was called the DynaTac and was the size of a brick! But it was not sold until ten years later. In 1983, cell phones finally went on the market.

The first cell phones were only used for talking and leaving voice mails. The Nokia 2110, released in 1994, was the first phone that could send and receive text messages. Texting was not popular at first. Americans each sent around 35 texts a month in 2000. But by 2007, texting was more common than calling!

DynaTAC

Nokia 2110

HOW IT WORKS

CELL PHONES

caller's voice   electrical signal

1. A cell phone changes the caller's voice into an electrical signal.

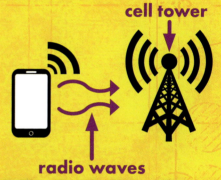

cell tower

radio waves

2. The electrical signal is sent by radio waves to the nearest cell tower.

3. A network of cell towers sends the radio waves to the receiver's cell phone.

4. The radio waves are changed back into an electrical signal and then into sound.

The first smartphone was invented in 1992. It was called the Simon Personal Communicator. This smartphone was large and bulky. People used a **stylus** to choose options on the touchscreen.

The late 1990s and early 2000s saw the release of sleeker smartphones. BlackBerry phones were the most popular. They had small screens and full keyboards. Users could **browse** the Internet and send emails. At the time, this was groundbreaking!

Simon Personal Communicator on charger

stylus

BLACKBERRY

Inventor's Name: A Canadian company called Research In Motion

Year of Release: 1999

Uses: The BlackBerry's full keyboard made sending emails easy. It was also one of the most secure phones on the market.

THE RISE OF SMARTPHONES

Smartphones leaped forward in 2007 when Apple introduced the iPhone. A year later, the first Android smartphone debuted. Both smartphones had touchscreens. They were also the first smartphones to feature apps.

2007 iPhone

Android T-Mobile G1

Smartphones have changed how people work, play, and communicate. Today, users take photos with **HD** cameras and store them in the **cloud**. Friends connect on social media websites. They use apps to edit photos, play games, and stream movies. Voice assistants, such as Siri and Alexa, answer questions and respond to commands. They can even tell jokes!

Smartphones play a large role in the Internet of Things, or IoT. The IoT is the system of devices that can connect to the Internet. Smartphone apps are often used to control these devices. Homeowners use smartphones to turn on lights. Athletes monitor their heart rates. Farmers check their fields. Smartphones make these tasks easy!

DID YOU KNOW?

Today's smartphones have more computing power than the Apollo 11 lunar module *Eagle*. This spacecraft was used to land on the Moon in 1969.

But smartphones can also cause harm. They can distract users while they walk or drive. This can cause accidents. Some people become **addicted** to their phones. They may pay more attention to their phones than to others. People must make sure to use smartphones safely.

A SMART FUTURE

Future smartphones will look different than today's phones. **Transparent** smartphones are in the works. Phones that stretch and fold may one day be common. **Ports** may disappear completely. Wireless charging will be the norm!

Galaxy Z Fold

Galaxy Z Flip

The use of smartphones in health care is growing. Among the biggest is the use of wellness apps. Every year, more of these apps become available to track health and monitor symptoms. **Telehealth** is also on the rise. Doctor visits on the phone are becoming more common. Telephones connect people and make lives easier!

TELEPHONE TIMELINE

1876
Alexander Graham Bell patents the telephone

1915
The first cross-country phone call is made in the U.S.

1885
AT&T is founded

1927
The handset is introduced

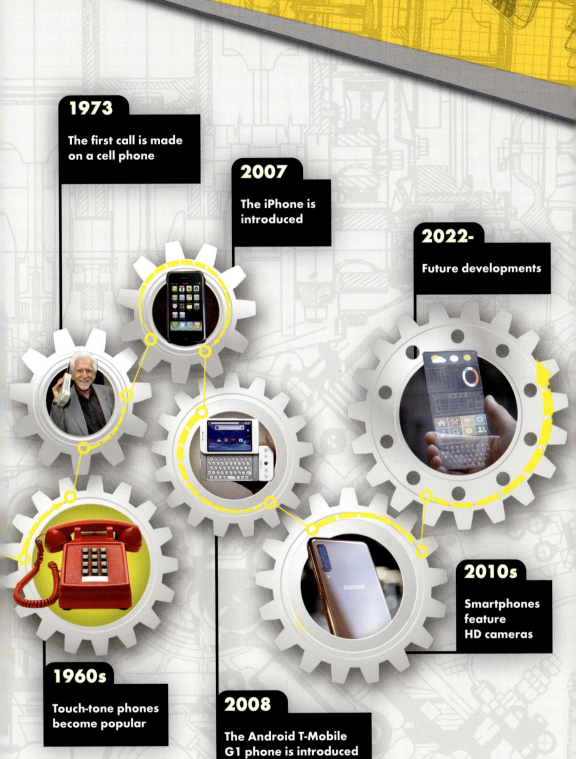

GLOSSARY

addicted—having a great need to do or have something

app—a computer program that performs special functions

browse—to examine things in a slow way

cellular phone—a wireless handheld device that uses radio waves to make and receive calls

cloud—the place on the Internet where information is stored

handset—a combined telephone transmitter and receiver mounted on a handheld device

HD—high definition; HD makes images that are sharper and more detailed than normal.

Morse code—a system of dots and dashes that stand for letters and numbers

operator—a person who directed calls for early telephone systems

patent—a document that gives an inventor the right to be the only one to make or sell their invention for a certain number of years

ports—physical connection points on computers or other electronic devices

receiver—the part of a telephone that changes electric currents into sound

rotary—able to turn

stylus—a pointed instrument used for writing

telehealth—technology used to provide health care and services

transmitter—a tiny microphone in the mouthpiece of a telephone's handset; a transmitter picks up sound waves and sends them over a wire.

transparent—clear enough to be seen through

TO LEARN MORE

AT THE LIBRARY

Coates, Eileen S. *Alexander Graham Bell's Telephone*. New York, N.Y.: PowerKids Press, 2019.

Colby, Jennifer. *Telephone to Smartphones*. Ann Arbor, Mich.: Cherry Lake Publishing, 2019.

Ward, Lesley. *Tech World: Cell Phone Pros and Cons*. Huntington Beach, Calif.: Teacher Created Materials, 2018.

ON THE WEB

FACTSURFER

Factsurfer.com gives you a safe, fun way to find more information.

1. Go to www.factsurfer.com.

2. Enter "telephone" into the search box and click 🔍.

3. Select your book cover to see a list of related content.

INDEX

American Telephone and Telegraph Company, 14, 17
Android, 22
app, 5, 6, 22, 23, 24, 27
Atlantic Ocean, 14
Bell, Alexander Graham, 12, 13, 14
BlackBerry, 20, 21
box telephone, 12
candlesticks, 15
cellular phone, 18, 19
cordless phones, 16
dials, 15, 17
Eagle, 25
Gray, Elisha, 12
handset, 15, 17
how it works, 19
Internet, 20, 24
Internet of Things, 24
iPhone, 22
Meucci, Antonio, 11
Morse code, 9, 10

Morse, Samuel, 9
Motorola Company, 18
operator, 10, 14, 15
patent, 11, 12
Pony Express, 8
ports, 26
Princess phone, 17
receiver, 12, 15
ringers, 12, 16
risks, 25
smartphones, 4, 5, 6, 7, 20, 21, 22, 23, 24, 25, 26, 27
social media, 23
telegraph, 9, 10, 11
telehealth, 27
text messages, 4, 5, 18
timeline, 28–29
touchscreen, 20, 22
transmitter, 12
United States, 8, 9, 14
Western Electric phones, 15, 16, 17

The images in this book are reproduced through the courtesy of: Issac Johnson, front cover (hero); Wiki Commons, front cover (small photo); cherezoff, front cover (left schematic); stefanphotozemun, front cover (right schematic); insta_photos, pp. 4, 6-7; Mr.Whiskey, p. 5; Pictures Now/ Alamy, p. 8; Jorge Royan/ Alamy, p. 9; INTERFOTO/ Alamy, p. 10; Leemage/ Getty Images, p. 11; Peter Horree/ Alamy, p. 12 (box telephones); Science History Images/ Alamy, p. 13; Circa Images/ Alamy, p. 14; Carmen Cristino/ Alamy, p. 15 (telephone left); ProhibitOnions/ Wiki Commons, pp. 15 (telephone right), 16 (telephone left); Retro AdArchives/ Alamy, pp. 17, 18 (telephone left); Vincent O'Byrne/ Alamy, p. 18 (telephone right); Bcos47/ Wiki Commons, p. 20 (telephone); Chris Willson/ Alamy, p. 20 (stylus); Natalia Bostan, p. 21; DMstudio House, p. 22 (iPhone); Mr.Mikla, pp. 22 (Android), 29 (Android); ThomasDeco, p. 23; Itsarapong Pokaew, p. 24; Just Dance, p. 25; Bhubeth Bhajanavorakul/ Alamy, p. 26; Syda Productions, p. 27; ArtMechanic/ Wiki Commons, p. 28 (Alexander Graham Bell); JHVEPhoto, p. 28 (AT&T); Rosseforp/ Alamy, p. 28 (first phone call); B Christopher/ Alamy, p. 28 (handset); Lawrence Roberg, p. 28 (touch-tone); WENN/ Alamy, p. 29 (first cell phone); marleyPug, p. 29 (iPhone); Karlis Dambrans, p. 29 (HD camera); HQuality, p. 29 (future phone).